PREDATORS

Jillian Powell

Editorial Consultants

Adria Klein

Cliff Moon

Lorraine Petersen

Frances Ridley

HAMERAY
PUBLISHING GROUP

Published in the United States of America
by the Hameray Publishing Group, Inc.

Published 2008

Author: Jillian Powell
Editorial Consultants: Adria Klein, Cliff Moon,
Lorraine Petersen, and Frances Ridley

Cover design: Button plc
Cover image: Alamy
Text design and typesetting: Andy Wilson
Publisher: Gill Budgell
Project management and editorial: Lesley Densham
Editing: Clare Robertson
Technical adviser: Mandy Holloway (NHM)
Illustrations: Chris King: pages 14–15, 24–25, 36–39
Photos: Alamy: pages 4–5, 6, 7, 8, 9, 11, 13, 16, 17, 18–19,
20, 22, 23, 26, 27, 28, 30, 31, 32–33, 34, 35, 40, 41, 43
Corbis: pages 6, 10, 12, 21, 23, 29, 42
Kobal: page 33

ISBN 978-1-60559-012-7

Printed in China.

1 2 3 4 5 6 7 IPS 22 21 20 19 18 17

Contents

Hunter and Prey 4

Killing Machines 6

Big Cats 8

Bears 12

A Snake at School – Part One 14

Pack Hunters 16

Snakes 18

Crocodiles 20

Spiders 22

A Snake at School – Part Two 24

Deadly Bugs 26

Ocean Predators 28

Killer Whales 30

Great White Sharks 32

Octopuses 34

A Snake at School – Part Three 36

Birds of Prey 40

Quiz 44

Glossary of Terms 45

More Resources 46

Answers 47

Index 48

Hunter and Prey

Predators are animals that eat other animals.

There are predators in the air, on land and in the sea.

Some are skilled hunters. Others lie in wait and **ambush** their **prey**.

If they don't eat, they die. It's life or death in the wild.

Killing Machines

Predators are designed to kill.

Sharp eyes

These help predators spot their prey before it spots them.

Eagle eyes see four times further than human eyes.

Powerful jaws

These help predators grip on to their prey and not let go.

A spotted hyena has the strongest jaws of any meat eater. It can even bite through bone.

Pointed teeth

Sharp, pointed teeth can slice into hides and meat.

Strong legs

Predators that hunt are built for speed.

A cheetah can go from 0 to 50 mph in three seconds!

Sharp claws and talons

Knife-sharp claws and **talons** grab and hold on to prey.

Secret weapons

Some predators have secret weapons. They use chemicals, poisons or **sonic** booms to stun their prey!

Big Cats

Big cats are big game hunters. They **stalk**, chase and jump to kill their prey.

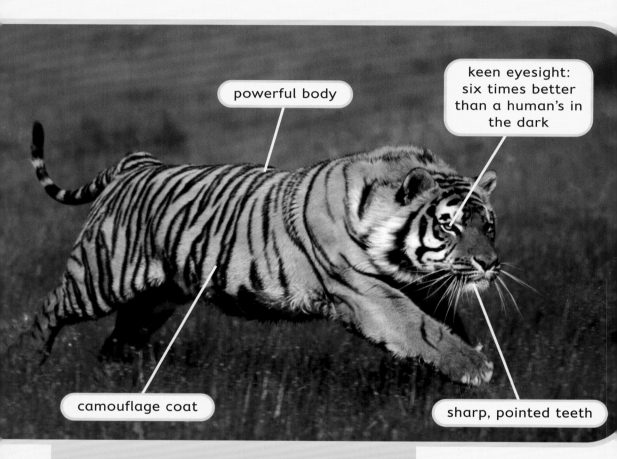

powerful body

keen eyesight: six times better than a human's in the dark

camouflage coat

sharp, pointed teeth

Tigers

Tigers are the largest cats.

Tigers can grow up to thirteen feet long, and weigh up to 800 pounds. They can bring down deer and bison.

Lions

Most big cats hunt alone, but lions hunt in groups and share their kill.

Only one in six chases ends in a kill. So lions aim for big prey like wildebeests and zebras.

Cheetahs

Cheetahs are the fastest animals on land.
They can run at speeds of up to 70 mph.

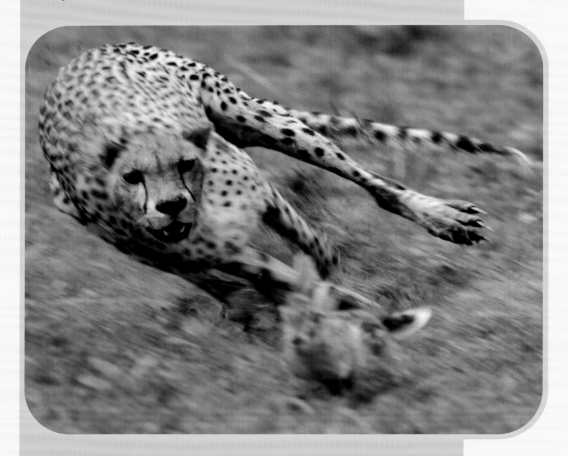

A cheetah grabs prey with its claws.
It knocks the prey down and kills it
by biting its neck.

At full speed, a cheetah covers
twenty feet with one stride.

All four feet are off the ground
for up to half the time!

Jaguars

Jaguars have powerful jaws. They kill prey with one bite.

They can climb trees to catch monkeys.

They can even drag fish out of water.

Leopards

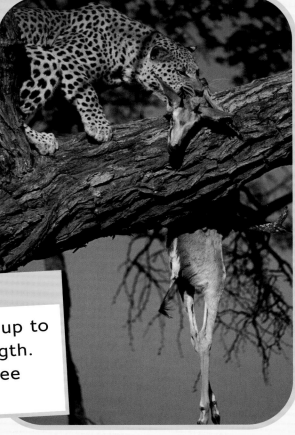

Leopards sometimes drag their kill up into a tree. This keeps it away from other predators.

Leopard facts!

Snow leopards can leap up to ten times their body length. They can strike prey three times their own size.

Bears

Polar bears

Polar bears are the biggest land predators. They are incredible hunters. They feed on seabirds, whales, seals and walruses.

Polar bears can smell prey from over 40 miles away.

They break the ice and pull prey out with their powerful claws.

Polar bear facts!

Height: up to 11 feet tall when standing.

Weight: up to 1,500 pounds.

They can eat 100 pounds of seal blubber in one meal.

Brown bears

Brown bears start a hunt by sniffing the air.

They circle their prey, then jump. They can knock down elk, caribou and moose.

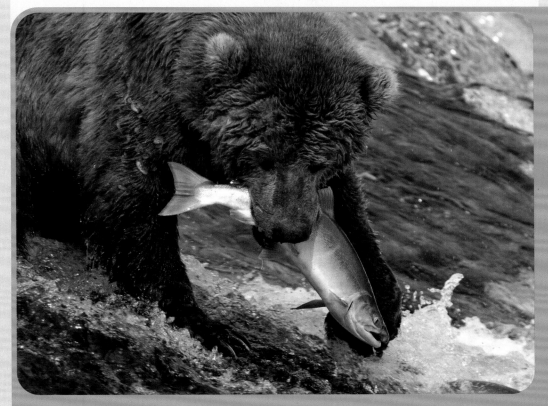

They are also skilled fishers.
They grab fish with their teeth or claws.

Brown bear facts!

A brown bear can stand ten feet tall and weigh up to 1,000 pounds.

A Snake at School
(Part One)

It was Bring a Pet to School day, and the school was raising money for charity.

Students would give short talks about their pets. The most popular pet would win a prize.

George and Darren read the rules.

"It just says all dogs must be on leashes," Darren said. "And caged animals must be kept in their cages."

"That's okay, then," George said. "I can bring Henry!"

"Are you crazy?" Darren said. "You can't bring a snake! You'll freak everyone out!"

"Exactly!" George said. "I can't wait to see the look on that Carla's face! Serves her right for turning down a date. And I want Henry to meet Todd Baxter. I'll show Todd for taking my place on the football team!"

Continued on page 24

Pack Hunters

Hyenas, wolves and wild dogs hunt in **packs**.

Hyenas

Hyenas hunt mainly by night.
They whoop when they get
together to hunt.

They track their prey by sight,
hearing and smell.

Hyenas eat every bit of an animal,
even its teeth and bones.

Wolves

Wolves eat the best parts of
a kill first. They hide the rest
in snow or ice.

This keeps it
fresh for later.

Snakes

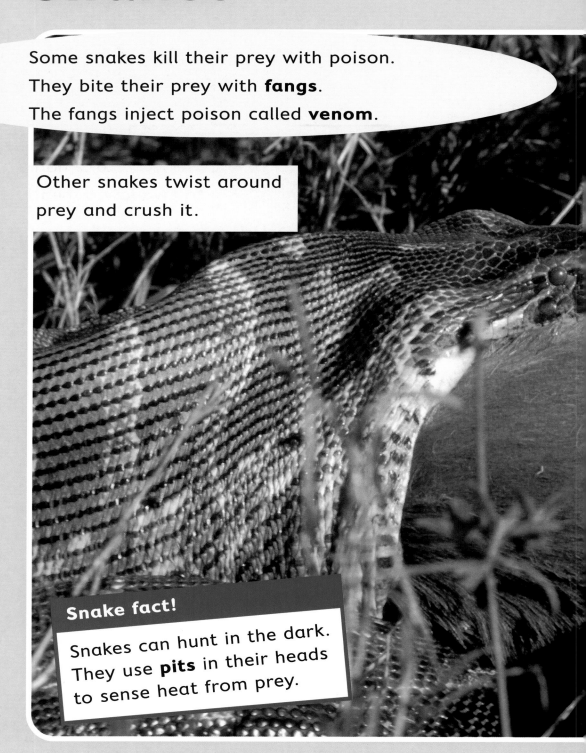

Some snakes kill their prey with poison.
They bite their prey with **fangs**.
The fangs inject poison called **venom**.

Other snakes twist around prey and crush it.

Snake fact!

Snakes can hunt in the dark.
They use **pits** in their heads
to sense heat from prey.

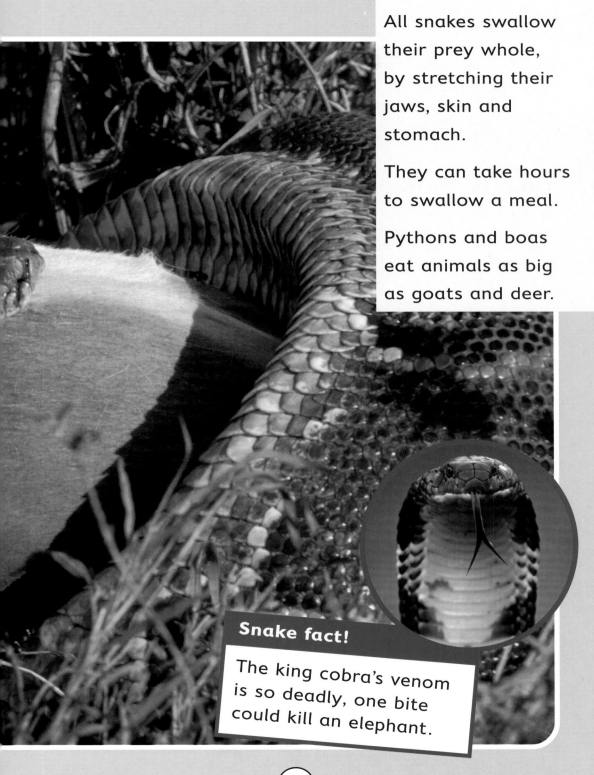

All snakes swallow their prey whole, by stretching their jaws, skin and stomach.

They can take hours to swallow a meal.

Pythons and boas eat animals as big as goats and deer.

Snake fact!

The king cobra's venom is so deadly, one bite could kill an elephant.

Crocodiles

Crocodiles lie in wait. Then they leap out of the water and grab their prey.

They are strong enough to pull a zebra into the water. They roll their prey over to drown it.

Sometimes, groups of crocodiles share a kill.

Crocodiles can grow up to twenty feet long.

They have over 60 large, cone-shaped teeth.

They have bone-crushing jaws
with a force of over
5,000 pounds per
square inch.

Crocodile fact!

Beware: on land,
a crocodile can sprint
at up to ten mph —
as fast as a human!

Spiders

Spiders ambush or hunt for their victims.

Some inject their prey with venom.
Other spiders trap their prey in webs.

Tarantulas ambush their prey.
They rear up and bite it with their
fangs. They inject venom and chemicals
which turn prey into liquid they can
suck like soup! Some tarantulas eat
birds, mice, frogs and lizards.

Spiders use many types of webs.

orb web

funnel web

Spider fact!

Spider silk is stronger than Kevlar – a material used for bulletproof vests.

Some webs are over 6 feet across. They are strong enough to catch birds or bats.

A Snake at School
(Part Two)

The classroom was buzzing. People had brought hamsters and rabbits. Carla's dog Benjy was there, with a bow on his head.

George was carrying a large sack.

"What's in the sack?" Todd Baxter asked.

George opened the sack. Henry's head appeared. Then his long body began to slither across the room.

Everyone began screaming. Todd jumped back in shock.

"A … a snake?" he gulped. "I mean, is it poisonous? Why is it putting its tongue out like that?"

"Just seeing what's around!" George grinned. "And no, Henry's not a **venomous** snake."

"Ugh! It's a disgusting slimy snake!" Carla said.

"He's not slimy. He's dry and cold. Look, feel him!" George held Henry up towards Carla. She was not impressed.

Continued on page 36

Deadly Bugs

Scorpions have a deadly sting in their tail.

Scorpions lie in wait under stones. Then they grab their prey with powerful **pincers**.

They use their sting to inject venom. Then they crush the prey to death.

Scorpion facts!

Some scorpions grow to 10 inches long. They prey on snakes, birds and lizards.

The praying mantis has a stick-like body. It uses **camouflage** to hide.

The mantis grabs its prey with its legs. These have hooks on them that help it grip.

Then the mantis bites off the victim's head!

Centipedes are fast movers.

Giant centipedes grow up to 10 inches long.

On their heads they have claws which inject deadly poison into their prey.

Cone snails are deadly sea snails.

Cone snails **harpoon** fish with venom.

Ocean Predators

The oceans are war zones.

Ocean predators use:

- shock attacks
- missiles
- camouflage
- chemical weapons
- sonic booms.

Box jellyfish or sea wasps have 5000 stinging cells on each **tentacle**. The jellyfish use the stinging cells as poison darts to shoot into prey.

Dolphins use sonic booms to stun their prey. They make bangs and clicking sounds which stun and confuse fish.

Venomous lionfish corner their prey using their large fins. They swallow it whole. Lionfish protect themselves from predators with spines that inject venom.

Killer Whales

Killer whales hunt like pack animals. They circle and herd their prey.

They send out sonic signals to find prey under water. The signals bounce off prey so the killer whales can 'see' it by sound.

Killer whales swim right up into the surf to catch seals or sea lions.

It takes years for a killer whale to learn this skill.

They can also break through ice to knock prey into the water.

Great White Sharks

Great white sharks are famous predators.

pointed snout

sharp eyesight

3000 sharp teeth

Great whites can swim at up to 25 mph. They hunt mainly by sight and smell. They often attack from below.

Great whites eat seabirds, seals, sea lions and fish. They even eat small whales and other sharks. About five deadly attacks a year are on humans.

streamlined body

Shark fact!

The film "Jaws" (1975) was about a man-eating great white shark.

Octopuses

Octopuses eat fish, crabs, turtles and other octopuses!

They have hundreds of suckers on their tentacles to grab victims. If they lose a tentacle, they just grow another!

They can confuse prey by squeezing out a cloud of black ink.

The octopus uses its sharp beak to bite and kill its prey. It takes the prey back to its den for a slow meal.

The world's largest octopus is the giant Pacific octopus. It can weigh over 150 pounds and have an arm span of 30 feet.

Octopus facts!

They have blue blood.

They have three hearts.

They can change shape and color for camouflage.

A Snake at School
(Part Three)

Henry was having a good time exploring.

"What does it eat?" someone asked.

"Dead mice," George answered. "We keep them in the freezer."

Everyone said "Yuck!"

"It's getting away!" Carla yelled.

"It's okay. He's gone in the PE cabinet!"
George said. "He'll like it in there. Lots of
things to climb over."

"Strange sort of pet!" Todd said. "But I
heard Jason Briggs in 5D has got a spider."

"Really?" George said. "Is it a tarantula?"
He went to see.

It turned out to be a large house spider in
a matchbox. But when George came back,
Henry had disappeared.

Continued on the next page

It was time for an assembly. Suddenly, everyone started screaming. They all ran for the door.

Henry was slithering across the stage. Then he disappeared through an open window.

George and Darren found him at lunchtime.

"Thank goodness!" Darren said. "No harm done!"

"I'm not sure about that!" George said. "Look at him!" He pointed to Henry's bulging stomach.

"Oh no! What's he eaten?" Darren said. "It could be someone's rabbit. It looks huge!"

Mrs Briggs appeared. She was one of the lunchtime supervisors. "That snake is a hero!" she smiled.

"Hero? He's eaten someone's pet!" Darren said.

"No he hasn't!" Mrs Briggs said. "He's eaten that rat that kept hanging around the trash bins. And you'd better go inside. He's just won Most Popular Pet!"

Birds of Prey

Birds of prey hunt from the air.
They use their powerful eyesight to find prey.

Some birds of prey can spot prey
hundreds of feet below. They dive
down to grab it with their talons.

Bird of prey fact!

Falcons can dive
at up to 180 mph.

The California condor is one of the largest birds of prey. Its wings have a span of nine feet. It has a sharp, curved beak and powerful claws. It hunts or **scavenges** for dead prey like cattle, sheep and rabbits.

Eagles

Eagles have the best eyesight of all. They can look to the front and sides at the same time.

Eagles can spot a rabbit moving from two miles away.

Eagles are powerful flyers.
They can carry off
a sheep or a deer.

The harpy eagle has talons as big
as a brown bear's claws.

They strike with twice the force
of a rifle bullet.

Quiz

1. Which predator has the strongest jaws?

2. Which big cats hunt in a group?

3. What are pack hunters?

4. How does a snake find its prey?

5. Name two ways spiders stop their prey from moving.

6. Which insect predator bites off the head of its prey?

7. How do killer whales find their prey?

8. How many teeth does a great white shark have?

9. How do octopuses confuse their prey?

10. Which predator has the best eyesight?

Glossary of Terms

ambush	To hide and attack by surprise
camouflage	To hide by blending in with surroundings
fangs	Long sharp teeth
harpoon	To strike with a sharp missile
pack	A group of hunting animals, such as wolves or hyenas
pincers	Arms or legs used like tongs
pits	Holes either side of a snake's head that can detect heat
predator	An animal that eats other animals
prey	An animal hunted for food
scavenges	Feeds on prey that is already dead
sonic	To do with sound waves
stalk	To follow and try to catch
talons	Claws of a bird of prey
tentacles	Arm-like or leg-like parts of a sea creature
venom	Poison
venomous	Poisonous

More Resources

Books

Polar Bears (Animal Predators)
Sandra Markle
Published by First Avenue Editions (ISBN-10:1575057460;
ISBN-13:978-1575057460)

Great White Sharks (Animal Predators)
Sandra Markle
Published by Carolrhoda books (ISBN-10:1575057476;
ISBN-13:978-1575057477)

Deadly Snakes
Andrew Solway
Published by Heinemann (ISBN-10:1403457727;
ISBN-13:978-15403457721)
(also: **Deadly Spiders and Scorpions** and **Birds of Prey**)

Magazines

Ranger Rick (National Wildlife Federation)
Award winning kids wildlife magazine packed with animal facts
and photos.

National Geographic Kids (National Geographic Society)
Read about animals, nature, and cultures from around the world
in this kids' version of a popular magazine.

Websites

www.nationalgeographic.com/animals
Amazing photographs, videos, fact sheets and wallpapers to
download on all kinds of animals including predators.

www.predatorconservation.com
The website of the Predator Conservation Trust, with lots of
information on predator animals around the world.

DVDs

Predators of the Animal World (1999)

National Geographic: Predators at war (2005)

Answers

1. The spotted hyena

2. Lions

3. Predators that work together to catch prey, like wolves and hyenas

4. By using pits in their heads to sense heat from the prey

5. Injecting them with venom or wrapping them in spider silk

6. The praying mantis

7. They send out sonic signals.

8. 3000

9. They send out an ink cloud.

10. The eagle

Index

ambush	4, 22	leopards	11
beak	34, 41	lionfish	29
bears	12–13	lions	9
big cats	8–11	octopuses	34–35
birds of prey	40-43	pack	16, 30
boas	19	pincers	26
box jellyfish	28	poison	7, 18, 28
brown bears	13, 43	polar bears	12
California condor	41	praying mantis	26
camouflage	26, 28, 35	pythons	19
centipedes	27	scavenge	41
cheetah	7, 10	scorpions	26
chemicals	7, 34	smell	12, 16, 32
claws	7, 12, 13, 27, 41, 43	snakes	14–15, 18–19, 24–25, 36–39
cobras	19		
cone snails	27	sonic booms	7, 28, 29
crocodiles	20–21	spiders	22–23
dolphins	29	spines	29
eagle	6, 42	stalk	8
eyes	6, 42	sting	26
eyesight	42	stun	7, 29
falcon	40	talons	7
fangs	18, 22	tarantulas	22, 37
great white sharks	32–33	teeth	6, 13, 21, 32
harpoon	27	tentacles	28, 34
hyena	6, 16	tigers	8
ink	34	venom	18, 22, 26, 27, 29
jaguars	11	webs	22, 23
jaws	6, 19, 21	wings	41
killer whales	30–31	wolves	16, 17